Self

7 Ultin

ссful in Life

By Sue Ellen

©Copyright 2016 WE CANT BE BEAT LLC

Copyright 2016 by Sue Ellen.

Published by WE CANT BE BEAT LLC

Krob817@yahoo.com

Table of Contents

Introduction 5

Chapter 1: What is success? 9

Chapter 2: Understanding Self-confidence and Self-esteem 14

    5 things you must know about self-confidence and self-esteem.. 18

Chapter 3: Getting Started 21

    What is Life? 21

Chapter 4: The Road block.. 26

Chapter 5: Discovering new ways 32

Chapter 6: New Scientific Discoveries in Technology 41

Chapter 7: Emotional Intelligence 45

    Study and Practice Emotional Intelligence for Occupation Development.. 45

Chapter 8:
Realistic Definition on Building a Sense of Humor .54

    How to Make Friends... 58

Fear of Failure and Fear of Success 63

Chapter 9: The Human Nature 70

Chapter 10: Persistence and Originality 84

Chapter 11: Getting Organized 96

Chapter 12: Indiscernible Laws and Their Tenacity 100

Chapter 13: The Real Success 105

The 7 Secrets behind Success 116

Conclusion 122

Introduction

Are you in a road block and want to be successful in life? Do you understand what real success is? You are not alone, many have found themselves in this dilemma. There are many untold secrets and queries regarding your future goals and ways of achieving these goals that must be answered. This book pulls you from the road block and sets a new start-over to transform your natural life on how you think via adding the points you were missing. Let's take a glimpse look on what you need to know as you begin; success!

What is success? Success is like a journey. We all want to be successful like entrepreneurs, businessmen, industrialists. We all want to be famous. We all want achievements. So if you want to span the road of success, you must understand the meaning of success. It's just like deciding the place where you want to go. There are so many beautiful places in the world but why does a particular place charm you? Similarly you have to understand that there are a lot of things you can achieve but what is the most important to you. What you think can make you one of those successful people? Once you interpret the meaning of success, half the battle is won. It's very important because unless and until you know where you want to go, you can't move ahead. After you've decided on a full-proof plan, pick up your bags and start moving towards your goals.

Now, once you have decided your destination, the next brightest thing would be to plan your journey and do the necessary exploration for it. Similarly, you have to sit back and do your goal setting. Your goals have to be in sync with the meaning of success you've discovered after questioning your inner self. Make a plan and be clear about how you want to go about to achieve your goals. Check out all the roads which lead to your destination and select the most feasible path. For every journey, you must be prepared for challenges (road blocks) before you reach your destination. How do you overcome them? In this case you need to have self-confidence!

What is self-confidence? It can be called a personal assurance that one has in themselves and their abilities. It is a vital trait that an individual possess that can be seen in the way they talk, their body language and in actions they take. It deals with the way individuals see themselves when it comes to their power, judgment, etc.

The attitude of a person towards themselves determines to a certain extent how they perform, how happy and how healthy they are in life. Personality starts building up from childhood experiences. Majority of it is influenced by how parents and vital people in your life treat you.

Children look for reactions from people around them in other to believe they are funny, safe, sheltered, intellectual and gorgeous. It is momentously pretentious via how a person thinks regarding other people around them think of them. Thus, this is backed when people have confidence in that what others say about them is how they are.

Many individuals base their degree of self-assurance on other people's judgment. If they contemplate that others have a boundless belief about them, they develop high esteem and if not, it becomes vice versa. The basis of peculiar appreciation is acquaintance and there is a method in which it can be erected. For you to have a strong self-belief do not miss learning about **the road block, new scientific discoveries, emotional intelligence, the human nature, indiscernible laws and their tenacity, and the real success**. Chapter one begins it all.

Chapter 1: What is success?

Success is such a complex word that when people say, almost half of the population in a certain country are successful while the information is so vague that they still have to define the real concept of success. This is because the word success can mean a lot of things and each denotation and connotation is dependent on the kind of situation and the turn of events. Success is something that is created and is not something that merely happen. For one to succeed first you should believe that you can and bring them into action as they are the foundations for any successive business. When you firmly believe in yourself, you can achieve anything otherwise you will find excuses. Most important thing is to surround yourself with good people as it is quite important to climb up the business ladder. This is like communicable, negative surrounding will block your success where as successful and goal-oriented individuals helps you to learn and take some of their habits to add to your own as you proceed along your road to success.

Nevertheless, success has a universal definition that people may use to define and to classify what is successful. Success is the progressive realization of a worthy ideal. Nevertheless, this simply means that people become what they think about. A person who knows where he or she is going, has a goal to aim, and an ambition to follow, then that is what success would mean. So to speak, if a person does not know where he or she is heading to, then, there are higher probabilities that the person will fail.

The Concept of Success

People, who are adept in linguistics and etymology of words, have tried to come up with the greatest definition they could ever give to success. But, after so many researches and psychological studies, the definition of success stand to be the progressive realization of a worthy ideal being the clearest and the most realistic definition. Simply to put the definition unto practice, it is clear that success starts from the day a person realizes what he or she wants to become and thinks of a way to pursue it.

The problem with most people who are buried deep with failure is that they tend to neglect the capability of their mind to foresee and project the things that they want to do. There are instances wherein some people keep on working hard and yet success seemed to be so far away. On the other hand, there are people who seem to be not exerting any effort at all and yet they achieve everything. It is from this point of view that others think that luck seems to be available to people who can afford to obtain them. It is like they have the powers of Midas touch, where everything turns into gold. It is like they have the world in the palm of their hand, ready to take the turns according to their fate and destiny.

The truth is that success befalls into people who have already set a long-term goal in their lives.

They have already set their mind to it, think about it day and night, and find the right time, place, and means to make it real. What they view with success is no longer a dream that usually lasts for hours only. What they see, from the start that they realized they want to do something and worked towards its realization, is a solid fulfillment of their dreams, something that they can touch and feel.

It is a great pity to people who fail to achieve their objectives in lives and yet continue to fail in spite of the hardships that they have gone through. This is because they fail to take charge of their thoughts. They neglected the fact that what they can do with their mind is exactly what they can do with their life. They fail to take their past life as an experience to future life.

These people who are constrained with failures are those who fall short of setting up a goal and focusing to find a way to reach that goal. Most important is to focus more on what an individual prerequisite in life. It is a simple mind-over-matter concept. It may not be easy at first but as you gradually program your mind to make it happen, it will surely happen.

In fact, other people contend that willpower is not solely an important factor in making things happen or in being successful. What it needs is programming so as to have direction and step-by-step process. Without direction, things will go astray. People should keep in mind that the human mind is such a powerful tool that it can even move innate things when initiated. Hence, never underestimate the power of the mind because it is the single and strangest secret to success.

Indeed, success is not owning everything like most people used to believe. Success is simply what you have set on your mind and the things that will follow will be the ways on making things into reality. You can also be successful and the means to achieve it is no longer a secret because everything will happen if you just put your mind to it.

Chapter 2: Understanding Self-confidence and Self-esteem

Self-confidence can be loosely defined as one's confidence in his/her own abilities, character and worth. It's not very unusual to find people who have very little, even none, of this. If you're one of those people who want to improve on their self-confidence, you have to know that it always starts on the inside. Work out the issues that you have that cause you to have low confidence in the first place. Once you have worked these things out, then you can work on the outside appearances.

Building Self-Confidence or Self-Esteem

Each of us has a reservoir of ability that we habitually fail to use. Failing to identify and develop our abilities contributes towards many of the inferiorities that we feel. By building self-confidence we can experience everything that we are and all we want to be. If you think about all your abilities, from tying your shoe laces, to driving a car, designing a building, making new friends or speaking in public, the one common element to all ability is frequent and consistent application of the same activity. The self confidence is gained in accordance with the knowledge and ability to perform any action.

So the key to building self-confidence is not some deep hidden ability that is unattainable to anyone. Achieving the level of self-confidence that we all want takes commitment, motivation and most of all consistent ongoing effort. You have to really want it, focus on specific areas and work towards the goals.

What's stopping you?

Doubts, fear and a lifetime of negative unproductive thinking keep us operating far below our capabilities. To release the inner strength needed to sustain the motivation to gain knowledge and practice the activities will involve some mental reprogramming. Taking those lifelong tired old unproductive negative thoughts and replacing them with powerful, success driven thinking.

You are probably asking yourself "What is he talking about?"

It is really nothing more than taking how you think and respond to any situation and conditioning yourself to think and respond in a different way (in a way that will help you achieve, prosper, and reach a desired goal).

Let's say that you would like to achieve a goal, like losing 20 lbs. Unfortunately every time you decide to begin a diet your old thinking patterns come into your head "It's not possible" or "I'll always be overweight" or "I can't change my eating patterns because there is no time to cook healthy meals". You can try to eliminate these harmful thinking patterns, but the real solution is to replace them with new ones. By installing the new attitudes and new beliefs, through repetition, you can retrain your mind to respond with thoughts and actions that will give you confidence and encourage you toward success.

Thus, this process will allow these new thoughts to be the dominate influence in your life. You will be one of the few people that will be able to tap into your inner reservoir of ability and project it at will. Building and sticking to self-confidence makes an individual naturally confident, sharp and more comfortable. There is just one other thing I would like to mention. It doesn't matter how young or old you are, you have the aptitude act on this. It does take a determined effort, our unproductive thinking patterns didn't happen overnight. Give it a chance to really become automatic. It's a proven method, very simple and will last a lifetime. I know that the change in you and your ability will not only affect your life, but will also have a positive direct influence in your family, friends and co-workers.

5 things you must know about self-confidence and self-esteem

Here are a few self-confidence tips that helps in gaining and making you to look more confident on the outside.

1. ***Walk and stand tall:*** Your presence affects how you look to other people, and whether we like it or not, other people's opinions of us still have an effect on our self-confidence, though it should not depend on it. When you stand and walk tall, you will actually look like you are confident, even during the times that you're not.
2. ***Try and improve your social skills:*** When you are more sociable, people tend to talk to you more as opposed to if you were always hiding in some corner just leering at everyone who passes by. Try to talk to people more, have a little chit chat here and there. It never hurts to ask someone how they are doing, even in passing. This will show that you are confident enough to put yourself out

there for people to talk to. And remember, a genuine smile on your face works better than expensive make up or clothes.

4. ***All articles that contain self-confidence tips will agree***: you have to be a go-getter. When people see that you have a drive to achieve your goals, they will take this as a sign of self-confidence, and will subsequently lead to them respecting you more.

5. ***Always be prepared***: This is especially useful in the workplace. When you are prepared for your work, let's say you have a presentation for your big corporate bosses, you will exude self-confidence because you know what you are talking about. It would be humiliating to be talking in front of very important people and suddenly draw a blank and just start mumbling in front of them. These kinds of situations can crumble your self-esteem. When you are always prepared, you will be able to conquer these fears and

speak of these things that you already know like the back of your hand.

6. ***The most practical of all self-confidence tips is this:*** work to make your body the way that you want it to be. In the looks department, it's no secret that some people are more fortunate than others. There are those that can eat and eat and not even gain a pound. If you're not one of these blessed people and you're not happy with how your body looks, then do something about it. There are so many gyms, sports and activities that you can do to become a better you. You can try boxing, biking or maybe even take up the art of Wushu. Either way, when you do something to get your body to the way you want it to look, you will definitely feel better about yourself and your self-confidence will begin to soar.

Chapter 3: Getting Started

It's ridiculous and amazing to all on what life is all about. People have different understanding and knowledge regarding life. There are theories based on biological findings, historic findings and the biblical findings which view life differently. May be all these could be true based on different factors. However, they confuse us and leave us hanging without being convinced. Thus, let us get started to understand what life is all about.

What is Life?

At some point in time every individual will ask themselves this question: "What is life all about?" Or something similar like: "Why am I here?" "Is there a God?" "Who created me or who created all this or where did it come from?" Many people blame God for everything bad that happens in their lives. Others blame the devil or just bad luck. Success guru's tell us they can show us how to figure everything out just pay them some money and they will show us how it all works and we will become amazingly happy under their guidance. Sounds good. Many people fall for that pitch and the next and the next. Hard on the old credit card. Addictive and expensive. Of course you feel great right after that amazing presentation. It takes a while to come back down to the real world. Your real world not their on stage fabrication world.

This book is not meant to kill any dreams or criticize those who are in the market place selling dreams. Does this include churches or religion? Of course it does. They compete head to head with these gurus for the hearts and souls of the populace. They all offer opinions and advice based on a system of beliefs. The key word here being belief. Napoleon Hill's book "Think and Grow Rich", claims that the common factor among the successful people is the belief that they have. "What the human mind believes the human mind can achieve". Even Christ advises that the Kingdom of God lies within each person. Many success guru's claim the secret is believing in yourself. Based on all these different but in many cases similar points of view it is obvious that this life is all about you and what you believe. About you and what you learn, what you accomplish and how you benefit mankind.

An old gentleman once told me "We are all the total sum of our past experiences." As a young man with limited knowledge I assumed that meant everything in a person's lifetime. Now older with more wisdom and understanding I have to acknowledge the possibility of many lifetimes. A known scholar by name Edgar Cayce claimed that, "a soul could hover over a body for some time deciding whether to live that life or not". He claimed that souls evolve over different lifetimes by overcoming adversity. Think of that for a minute. We have all heard the saying "If it doesn't kill us it makes us stronger". Without adversity would we have any accomplishments? The people we most admire and respect are those who overcome adversity. These are the people whose lives and accomplishments are recorded in the history books. Are aware what we miss or lack in life for these to take place? Self-confidence and self-esteem.

Does it really matter if there is a God to judge us? To be responsible to? Are we not responsible to society, our families and ourselves? Believing in God makes him real to you. So why care what someone else says or believes in? What you believe becomes your reality and becomes your life. If you want to be a Christian be a Christian. If you want to be a Muslim be a Muslim but be a good Christian be a good Muslim. Do not judge other faiths. Stand up for goodness and fight evil. Convert by example not argument or violence. Believe in God whatever you conceive him/her to be and strive to be good. There is a biblical saying from the book of Job that states "Wisdom is fearing the Lord and understanding is avoiding sin." Not complicated. Something every mother tells her children no matter the faith. Here you cannot fear God if you do not believe in him. We have already seen that what we believe in is what determines what we become and therefore how our life can be defined. A strong believer is likely to have much self-confidence or self-esteem.

So, "What is Life All About?" Quite simply your life is all about you. What you believe. What you accomplish. What you do for your fellow man. Why not make it a good life? Why not accomplish all you can? Why not help your fellow man? Then at the end of the day you can honestly say "Well Lord I did my best." Have no regrets because at the end of this life you will be your worst critic not God. You see He does truly love you and if anyone's love is unconditional it would be God's. We can build great confidence through God. A successful life denotes how much you believe in yourself and how you practice what you believe in. But always remember success does not come without road blocks. What are road blocks?

Chapter 4: The Road block

Every person in life has in one way or the other tried many ways to become successful. Nevertheless, we find ourselves not achieving our goals or objectives. The greatest query is, what is the major hindrance to success? *Road block* is the key word. What are our roadblocks to success? Have we discovered them or we are yet to? Either way, we can define the word road for clarity and more understanding.

What is a road block?

A road block can be an obstacle, an idea or imagination, a plan or anything else that hinder ones' success. Success calls for understanding, planning, self-confidence, motivation, self-esteem and a belief. Let take a shocking glimpse regarding several road blocks.

Failure to take responsibility of one's own actions.

Have you realized that when we fail to do our duties or make the right choices we influence our success in one way or the other? In most instances, people blame each other for their own mistakes that they could have avoided by making correct decisions or doing their duties appropriately. By a great percentage, our choices can be barriers or road blocks of success to us. Life involves too much of decision making and critical thinking so as to achieve what is required. Decision making must involve critical thinking always.

Convert to menace antagonistic as an alternative to running for the big profits on engagement

In business it is advisable to take control of the profit you expect in every business. When we magnify the profits we expect, it become practically impossible for our buyers and that may lead to great losses therefore, closing business or failure to make any sale. For profitable engagements, it is advisable to take averse risks while still taking smaller profits on long time basis. Therefore, this builds the business steadily.

In addition, never let anything to shake your self-confidence. Note that this is possible by managing your self-esteem or self-confidence. Always ensure, you are not blocked due to lack of knowledge in what you are undertaking at that moment.

Dearth of knowledge and experience

Like stated, success depends on habit, belief, passion, flexibility and attitude of an individual. Never dream for success, work for it. The real success of business is enthusiasm. Unless or until you have that urge you can't succeed. To be successful in business you must be courageous. You need to act smartly and try to think beyond your aptitude. Doesn't matter whether you succeed or fail you will learn a lesson and grow. Unfortunately we are blocked from success due to lack of knowledge and experience when it is necessary.

Lack of self-confidence and self-esteem

For one to succeed, you should first believe that you can and bring them into action as they are the foundations for any successive business. When you firmly believe in yourself, you can achieve anything otherwise you will find excuses. Most important thing is to surround yourself with good people as it is quite important to climb up the business ladder. This is like communicable, negative surrounding will block your success where as successful and goal-oriented individuals helps you to learn and take some of their habits to add to your own as you proceed along your road to success.

Lack of passion and failure to accept challenges

Accept the challenges as it is essential for any type of business success. It create your growth and direct you towards new business opportunities. Be selective, think deeply and intelligently on all your business requirements and concentrate on executing your business goals. There is no guarantee for success in business. Unknown is always looming, so it would be better to take risk and know your path. You won't get what you want if you don't take risk. Last but not least, do what you love or are passionate about. You will find more success when you do your lovable work and make your career in your passionate field. When you love the business you do it will help you to grow and achieve your desired goal. For you to fight challenges, you have to accept and evaluate their weight against you or they will block you from your goals. Love what you do so that you can be self-motivated and have morale in doing your business.

There are many road blocks that lead us astray, it is vital to discover and evaluates what precludes us from what we have always wanted to become. Note that load blocks can be anything including individuals who fights against your success. Nevertheless, most important be courageous and fill encouraged in your endeavors. Are you ready to make new discoveries?

Chapter 5: Discovering new ways

Life calls for change and commitment. You have to believe and be firm to be happy and lead a healthy, happy and a successful life. Every person may seek on how to lead a happy life. It's simple and very vivid in its ways.

How to lead a happy life

In this century of real misapprehension, we tend to gain real happiness only through material contentment. However, researches prove that happiness could not be attained only through fulfillment of material desires like a new car or new home. In fact, happiness achieved through materialistic gains is short-lived and go past quickly. Thus, this means if we actually wish to be happy, we got to change our attitude towards our success via achieving harmonization ourselves. As per the current findings conducted, real contentment is laid in recuperating the following characteristics that we already possess but fail to identify them.

1. Optimism: Whatever circumstances you might be living through, it is important to maintain a positive outlook towards life. Develop belief within yourself that you are worthy of achieving the best that life can offer you.

2. Courage: You needs to have the courage to defend your faith and belief. The faith and courage to change your destiny.

3. Practicality and ingenuity: People who love life always search for new ventures and are not afraid of trying new things. Even if they fail, they do not get disappointed and keep trying till they achieve success.

4. Self-confidence: Whatever you do, you need to feel confident and sure about it. Do not allow doubt to overshadow your prospective of achieving your goals through hard work and dedication.

5. Sound Health: So as to achieve true happiness, the mind, body and soul should be in harmony with each other. When you are physically fit, you

will be in a great frame of mind. Practicing Meditation regularly can unite our body, mind and soul.

6. Humanity: When you help others without expecting anything in exchange then you tend to experience a sense of happiness that come from within.

7. Love: When you love somebody, be it your beloved, your parents, or any of your near and dear one, you tend to develop a feeling of compassion and sympathy, which allows you to experience real happiness.

8. Set Goals: When you set achievable goals for yourself; you have something to concentrate upon. Something which gives meaning and purpose to your life. Therefore, this shall offer us a real pleasure when we successfully accomplish our goals.

If you wish to experience real happiness then it is none other than you who can bring happiness to your life as you have the control over your happiness even more than you might have actually imagined.

Clear the obstacles on your way

There are many factors that may keep you from changing yourself enough to find success. Yes, I did mention change because if what you are doing today is not working chances are you will have to change to find the success you seek. You can be as successful as anyone else, but first you need to identify what is holding you back so that you can change it and move forward to success.

Fear is probably the biggest factor holding people from success today. Most of us are not willing to take any risks to be successful. Now I am not saying you should stake your financial future and put a second mortgage on your home to be successful, but neither am I saying you shouldn't. If the goals and your commitment are big enough you have to do what it takes to get you there.

Fear is usually a matter of not understanding something enough. Educate yourself on every aspect of what you want to do, understand what it takes to be successful in your field and then DO IT. Make sure that you understand it as well as you can, this will help alleviate fear. Lack of knowledge about your field can lead to failure. Focus on the things you can change, or influence and work in those areas. Fear of things you cannot change is simply a waste of your time. Take action and start to move forward. Advance on the fear daily and it will begin to retreat.

Pressure from family and friends is another thing that can really hold someone back. Family and friends have a great meaning and sometimes they can advise us and "save us from our own mistakes". Consequently, most of the time when we share our ideas with family and friends they get scared with us because we are so excited and they advise us against the venture because they don't want to see us hurt. They are a great meaning, but if you ought to be successful, you must be able to either keep your distance from the negative people. Alternatively, look for them in the face and thank them for sharing and move ahead with your decision without letting their fears poison your excitement and ambitions.

Do not allow others to make your decisions for you unless they are where you want to be. If you want to find success you will have to change what you are doing and go against what they are doing. Make a stand for yourself. Since you have always done something a certain way and it worked reasonably well you are comfortable with it, but if it's not getting you the results you really want you may have to break the mold and do something a lot different to find success.

Most people have habits that keep them from being successful. Be willing to break those habits and replace them with new more profitable ones. It takes 21-30 days to develop a new habit. Make a commitment to change just one thing a month and you will see improvements immediately. If you want different results you are going to have to take different actions.

How much do you really want to be successful? Do you really care? Lack of true commitment is a real killer for success. You may think it sounds great to make lots of money every month, but doing what it takes to get there is another thing altogether. Do you really care enough to make a commitment, take action and get things moving? This is crucial to your success. You need to really take a look at your current situation and decide if you have what it takes to be successful or if you just have what it takes to dream about being successful. There is a big difference between those two.

Do you see yourself as successful? If you see yourself negatively you will have a tough time overcoming that and being successful. Make a list of what you want to be and then turn those things into positive statements about yourself. Your list may look like this:

I am motivated.

I am organized.

I am decisive.

I am successful.

I am educated.

I am happy.

You get the idea from that list that it can include anything you wish to be. Start going over that list and change the habits that will make those statements true and say those true statements to yourself. This will change your mindset and your success will increase as you begin to see yourself as successful. When you start seeing yourself as successful others will see that too.

No matter what you do for work if you are willing to change yourself and do whatever it takes you will be successful. Being successful takes action, not just wishful thinking. Expect opposition and handle it so that you can keep moving forward and create a successful future for you and your family. When you are willing to make changes in your life to move toward success you cannot help but find it. Take the first step today! See what is happening with scientific world.

Chapter 6: New Scientific Discoveries in Technology

In general, there are many scientific discoveries that have been made. In all the newly made adventures, technology is involved by around 98%. These discoveries vary depending on the field of specialization for example, in engineering, medicine, soil science, computer science or agriculture among others. Today we must accept that we are driven by technology in whatever we do and the world has been changed completely via technology. What can technology do? Does it strengthen your self-esteem?

Ways of Embracing Technology to Gain Self-Confidence

Technology can enhance the accomplishment of many project when positively used. Good companies know that education is important, if you want to be current with the newest technology and business ideas. You can learn through traditional methods like classes, training sessions, conferences, and trade shows. However, these traditional methods take a lot of time that a busy company owner might not have.

Another choice to consider in the business world is hiring mental coaches. These coaches usually have a lot of experience in management and have a lot of useful knowledge. These coaches are already a success in the business world, and this gives them a lot of useful experience to fall back on. A lot of coaches are available all day and night so as to work with the company's busy schedule.

Majority of life coaching centers offer mental coaches which outfit their services to a different role in a company's organization. Some examples are information technology, human resource management, financial management, or logistics. Many also have services available for the executives of the company like the President or CEO.

Mental coaches cater to specific areas of expertise and industries. Locating mental coaches that match your budget as well as the skills you want to develop, begin searching the internet for business organizations that focus on your area of expertise. Next, search online testimonials from other professionals in your field and network with colleagues for information or references. Lastly, check with your supervisor. Chances are that the partaker already has experience in mental coaches or can connect you with someone who has.

Businesses know that employees are more efficient when they have been trained properly. A lot of companies will hire coaches, or reimburse the employee for the costs. Check with your supervisor to be sure that the coaching sessions meet your company's rules for being reimbursable before you sign up for coaching.

Recognizing potential while owning the attitude of self-confidence, business owners employ coaches to teach and often revive these mental skills so that their company is seen as sharp and able to hold their own when either expanding overseas or seizing the growth opportunities in their current industries and markets. Business owners and executives know, at the end of the day that increases in the bottom line are a direct result of the mental fortitude that comes from realized potential.

To be a success in business, you have to keep up with the latest methods and techniques in your profession. Another way that businesses are becoming more competitive is by enlisting the help of mental coaches for their employees. To find coaches that best fits your needs and budget, search the internet for business organizations that cater specifically to your area of expertise. You might also choose to look for a life coaching institute. Because companies are aware that a well-trained employee is a better employee, many have chosen to pay for coaches, or reimburse costs once the coaching is completed successfully. Note that your emotions or attitudes play a great role in your success.

Chapter 7: Emotional Intelligence

Study and Practice Emotional Intelligence for Occupation Development

Emotions constitute an important part of a person's personality. If unregulated, consequences will be costly, fatal and often result in loss of career, reputation and business. Emotional intelligence is highly connected with self-control that contribute to one's success in leadership roles. Emotional intelligence can be defined simply as 'regulation of emotions keeping in mind how it affects people around you'. Emotional intelligence is a prerequisite for promotions and people with emotional intelligence can be trusted with client facing and diplomatic tasks.

Studies have revealed that people with high emotional intelligence rise in the ranks against people with low emotional intelligence. Howsoever intelligent a person be, if that person lacks emotional intelligence he will go one step forward and two steps backward as his unregulated emotions cause problem for others resulting in the breaking of team. This is one of the reasons why recruiters are looking not just IQ but commensurate EI (Emotional Intelligence) to support his IQ for job.

Self-awareness' is the most important thing to understand one's emotions, how controllable and uncontrollable are emotions in different and difficult situations. Awareness about one's emotion enable one to take pro-active steps to keep emotions under check. If knowing about one's emotion is the first step, knowing about others emotions is the second step. This will help in empathizing with the feelings and emotions of others for stronger bonding,
and well cemented relationships. If one is successful in empathizing with others, he will be in an advantageous situation to manage relationship and use them effectively. People who are expert in empathizing can successfully

build large organizations.

Emotional intelligence applications

Emotional intelligence can be applied in multiple spheres. People want to be affable, sociable and they want elevation in their respective career fields. Moreover, business relationships need cementing and family bonds require nurturing.

Everything starts from family. Family is the first place to cultivate emotional intelligence. Between man and wife there should be peace and harmony. This can be achieved only by expressing empathy to the other person when they are emotionally weak. Habit of forgiveness and putting things behind past are absolutely essential for nurturing healthy family bonds. This will have its reflection in social as well as professional life.

When it comes to social life especially in dealing with others one should show his emotional intelligence through his listening skills. This requires patience and of course empathy. These two qualities see other person's needs and enable one to react with tact and concern. The same expressions should be extended to oral as well written communications where the empathy should be well reflected.

In professional life, we deal with strong people and weak people. Some will be high skilled but with low emotional intelligence. Look at a few others, they will not be high performers but average performers but having high emotional intelligence. Here comes empathy to identify his weak areas to give proper training aimed at improving productivity. Such ones will be loyal to the company and will bring laurel to 'you' the leader who trained that person.

There are many theories in emotional intelligence. Very few areas were mentioned for the sake of information. To understand more, it is highly recommended to attend intelligence courses from a reputed institute. Online intelligence training courses are also available for those who look for distance education. Attend one such course to redefine your family and social life.

Understanding Others via Emotional Intelligence

People think no one knows them like the way they do. People maintain that they are more familiar with their houses than anybody else is. They assert that they have far more knowledge about their neighborhood when compared with others. People just like to profess that they understand their lives inside out. On the other hand, with regard to emotions and personalities, the truth is quite contrary to what is stated. We are inclined to turn a blind eye with regard to our own failings. We would like to believe that we are aware of our emotions and personalities really well, but the fact is that a majority of people overlook their own shortcomings.

For instance, let us take emotional intelligence. When a person gets to know about the significance of EI, without much ado, he starts to dwell on people whom he feels are bereft of emotional intelligence. Actually, not many people take the trouble to look at themselves to find out if they are devoid of EI.

It is for this reason that a person requires to undergo intelligence tests. Now, a person should understand simply to what extent the matter of emotional intelligence tends to shape his life. The best possible way to make someone realize his limitations is to cause them to become conscious of it themselves. Now, if somebody came near you just now and stated that you were without EI, is it possible for you to accept it as true?

A person has to be presented evidence regarding his failings before he is convinced. The advantage of tests on emotional intelligence lies in the fact that these tests give you an opportunity to confirm simply how right you were about the observation of yourself. By going through a test on emotional intelligence, you may expose yourself to the likelihood that you do not just know yourself the way you believe you do.

This alteration in assessment makes it easier for you to modify your way of thinking with the intention that you become more aware of the need to change for the better. A further benefit of undertaking a test on emotional intelligence is that it makes it possible for a person to identify exactly that particular portion of emotional intelligence that he is found wanting. By means of a test on emotional intelligence, it is possible for a person to gather as to which section of emotional intelligence needs his attention.

Emotional intelligence tests, in addition, make it easy for someone to appreciate the prospect of possessing emotional intelligence. By way of these EI tests, a person discovers how to avail himself of emotional intelligence, each day of his life. Due to this, a person can lead a far more contented and successful life. Moreover, emotional intelligence tests too can enlighten a person just to what extent he is able to connect with other people. Now, social interface can prove to be enormously significant in one's life. This is dead right. You could be either an employee or a student, but you definitely require others to lend a hand as you travel down life's way.

Tests on emotional intelligence can assist you to improve your aptitude and sense of the way other people feel. Therefore, this aptitude enables you to identify yourself with those around you. Insight is the basis of knowledge. When you are capable of securing some awareness about a person's emotions, then you should not have any difficulty in counting him as part of your inner circle. Tests on emotional intelligence are wonderful since they permit a person to observe the facts. It is common knowledge that the utmost barrier to truth is found in one's self. A test on emotional intelligence can negotiate a person's resistance and permit that person to assess himself without prejudice.

Chapter 8:
Realistic Definition on Building a S ense of Humor

Who says there is no single cure for all of life's problems? There is, and it is called humor. Yes, the ability to laugh in the face of the very situation that gave you the blues is powerful, and addictive! Humor is the cushion that can soften the impact of many shocks, and not let the minor ones even register. Sadly, even though people understand the importance, they are at a loss at how to make it happen in their lives.

Gelotology is the study of laughter, and as such can encompass a consideration of the philosophical bases for humor. Nevertheless, gelotology is mainly concerned with the act of laughing itself, however, and in particular all its psychological and physiological aspects. Though gelotological research has been conducted, its primary motivation is of a therapeutic and practical nature.

For theories of laughter and humor in general, we remain with the philosophers and other such "cultural thinkers." Whatever humor is, it is generally agreed to be a gift from God, a blessing, for it is tough to imagine a life without having laughter, which is to say a person without a sense of humor. And as hard as it would be to explain just what humor is, it's even harder to explain why it is - although the two might well be related. For instance, some evolutionary psychologists view humor as a means of sexual selection by females, as an indicator of other traits, for instance intelligence, that do confer obvious survival benefits.

Definitely, aptitude seems somehow convolutedly linked to a nous of humor as in the old line about "he who laughs last.., thinks slowest." Humor appears rather intricate, but certain traits appears alike: An unsuitableness, a misattribution, even feelings of preeminence. All these necessitate a human being (often regarded as the only innate that laughs), a configuration recognizing sense-making creature.

What makes something funny often goes against our preconceived notions (incongruity), or allows us to make light of serious issues (misattribution), or can even be due to a feeling of advantage (superiority). Thus we laugh if somebody shows up for work wearing a suit and tie with his pants' zipper unzipped; we find the sight of a man falling out of a building flailing crazily, as if trying to fly, strangely funny; we may even snicker at a homeless panhandler mumbling to himself over a can of beer.

Humor is Useful in Daily Life and Not Just in Comedy Shows

People usually relate humor to the antics performed by a strange guy in funny pants on a TV show on weekends. Well, not quite - there is a world of difference between humor and laughter. While you may not be displaying the full set of your teeth to the world all the time, it is important to maintain the funny disposition. Here is how you can go about doing it:

Surround yourself with humor: You need to make an effort to ensure that the river of humor keeps flowing in your life. Maybe it is some very witty comedian you admire, or a humorous writer you enjoy - make sure that you take out some time daily and a lot of time weekly for it. This will perpetuate happiness and light-heartedness in your life and will help you keep your cool in trying situations. Believe it or not, no medicine is permanent (except poison!) - You need to keep up the regular practice of being humorous to derive some benefits.

Get motivated, in a funny way: There is no better and practical way than to learn this art hands-on. Therefore, it is indispensable to find a teacher who can drive you to achieve more by the application of humor. You can read all the books that you want in the world, but if humor is not learned practically, only failure will have the last laugh! Do not keep waiting any longer. Experience the power and effectiveness of humor in your life, and discover how easy it is to laugh your way to happiness and success!

How to Make Friends

The first successful mission in life is making friends. Friends motivate and encourage each other, brings self-confidence and exchange of knowledge. You need to know how to make friends. Your social life is not going anywhere fast. Your colleagues talk animatedly about all the social events they have been to last weekend or the ones coming up next. You live in horror of the inevitable question "So, what are you doing next weekend then? You wish with all your heart that you knew how to become the guest that everyone wants to invite to their barbeque, pot luck dinner, on a double date, a picnic or something more formal.

Are you one of those people who do get invited but find that you are not asked back for a second time? It doesn't have to be painful to impress people you want to see more of. It doesn't have to be you spending weekends alone. If you practice these easy tips on how to have successful conversations.

Firstly, cultivate conversation starters. Once you start, you will find that a whole new world will open up to you. Firstly, open conversations with everyone you meet. The counter clerk at your local convenience store, the desk jockey at the library, the sales assistant at the hardware store, the wait staff at your favorite café, the person standing next to you at the bus stop or travelling in the bus or train with you. Get the picture?

This technique works amazingly well with people you meet in the course of buying something. Wait until they are half way through serving and then simply ask "How are you doing today?" Nevertheless, this is an extremely effective way to connect. The key here is to wait, then ask. This approach will cause the person serving you to pause and look at you and really engage. And then all you have to do is listen and ask questions as they cue you in! Easy as! And guess what? The more you do this, the more opportunities that will open up for you to strike up conversations. People often want to keep talking even though they have other customers waiting!

Another area to work on is being aware of how the other person sees you. That is, your body language. Practice looking people in the eye, smiling when you ask how they are, nodding when they respond and focusing on what they are saying. If you feel nervous or shy, then I always say "fake it till you make it"; that is act as if you are confident. Spend some time every day visualizing how successfully you will talk to people and feel how good it is to connect with people. This will help enormously.

Once you have mastered this art, people will want to talk to you. Your work colleagues will notice you in a different way and you will begin to get invitations to social outings. To be someone who gets invited back again and again there are some things to remember about what to do and how to participate throughout the event.

Put your best foot forward. Dress your best and for the occasion. This means if it is casual, wear casual clothes - but your best casual outfit. If it is formal then dress formally. If it is a relaxed event, then arrive on time. Don't get there 15 minutes early when your hosts are still rushing around organizing things. This is awkward. If it is something more formal, then you can arrive a few minutes before the stated time as this will help you to orient yourself.

While you are there, introduce yourself to people and use your expertise in starting and conducting conversations. Socially confident people introduce information about themselves earlier in the conversation. Don't wait for the other person to ask your name. Introduce yourself early and ask for their name. Then use it. They say we need to say something five times aloud before we truly remember it. So remember to use their name when you ask them a question. Follow up with a question about them like those listed below and look for interests in common.

Here are some tips to move the conversation into more and more personal levels:

- Use the environment. Make a comment about your surroundings.
- Share little things about recent events; movies, new cafes you have tried.
- How about a book you recently read; ask what interesting books they have read.
- Keep up with current events and share these: news, sports, and community events.
- Ask open ended questions beginning with what, where, when.
- Remember to listen and be enthusiastic about what you are hearing.
- Give compliments about an article of clothing and ask where they got it.

- Relax, make eye contact and shake hands when you meet.
- Recall previous conversations you may have had with the same person and ask for an update or if things have changed or what has happened since you last met
- Finally, if things are dragging let the conversation go. You won't connect with everyone.

Keep an eye on how the event unfolds and take cues for when it might be time to leave from others. Remember, always thank the hosts and don't gush. A simple thank you for a lovely time, or "thank you for organizing this, I had a great time" will be enough. Only offer to help if you can see this would be appropriate. A rule of thumb is the more formal the occasion, the less this would be seen as the right thing to do.

Fear of Failure and Fear of Success

A certain team manager stated that, "of all the conversations I have facilitated via coaching in the past 10 years it astounds me the amount of people who divulge either one on one or in a seminar format that they have a fear of either failure or success!" I personally do not believe as a spiritual being you can fail so do not buy into this belief. It saddens me how many people state this and yet are not present to the costs of where they are resonating.

I heard a fabulous quote and I am sorry I cannot remember the person who wrote this but I feel it sums up what I believe success means. Here it is:

"Success should not be measured by your achievements alone, it should be measured by the obstacles that you have had to overcome". Logically why would a person in their 30, 40, 50's continue influencing their world by stating they have a fear of failure unless they were committed to sabotaging their reality? Beliefs are almighty powerful and can make or break a dream. If you are interested in transformation and have a fear of failure check out how ludicrous this is!

People rattle it off like ordering a 'flat white coffee', no consciousness around how debilitating this belief/fear is. Then to the contrary I also hear people state that they are fearful of success, doubly ludicrous. How's that for complete and utter sabotage. Just because you have a belief does not mean it has any reality, have you ever thought about that? People are so had by their feelings, especially their default, disempowered feelings that they do not interrupt this thought patterning. When you state you are afraid of failure, or afraid of success, what does it actually mean? It is usually stated in such a sweeping statement that most people are not present to the impact of such statements. They state it like a finite statement.

You possess the knack to discipline your contemplations and if this is the case then you also have the power to re-create your future by changing the way you think. I do not believe you need to overcome these fears for fear has no reality but the reality and meaning to which you give it. Fear is but a barometer of your disconnection from yourself/faith and is only but a projected thought, either past or future related. Nothing more, nothing less. I could write a whole blog article on living a fearless existence, now there's an idea!

Are you suggesting anything?

Top 10 Tips for Ending Fear Of Failure/Fear of Success Paradigm

1. Check out how funny these contrasting statements are and commit to a future where you will no longer operate from this resonance.

2. When you frame the statement, ' I am fearful of Failure/Success', distinguish in that moment where the projection is coming from, past or future? Once distinguished get present to the costs in that moment of being a self-fulfilling prophecy of self-sabotage.

3. Worst case scenario: If you are so attached to the habit of experiencing these fears, go there, future pace your life, 5, years, 10 years, 20 years from now continuing to make these statements, what impact do you think these negative affirmations will have on your future?

4. Create a powerful affirmation to counteract these negative affirmations. Now I am not one for affirmations unless they are used repeatedly for the purposes of retraining/reprogramming old thought patterns. So unless you are willing to be disciplined in this regard, forget it.

5. You are the adult, note that whenever you frame in your language "I am fearful of failure or successes, in that moment you are operating from the wounded child - see a healer and work on your childhood conditioning.

6. Procrastination is often bred from a fear of failure. Imagine your life where you end procrastination in your life for good, get present to that! Fear of anything usually is used as unconscious and in some cases conscious

mechanism to keep you disempowered. Perfect strategy from the default!

7. When you do not accomplish something, some people may view this as being a failure. Personally speaking why do we default to the negative connotation? Why do we not automatically default to the more empowered connotation of being courageous enough to have given it a go where others have feared to tread?

8. Turn within when you are fearful, ask what love would do in this moment and chose love over fear, not a new concept but an often forgotten one.

9. Embrace having compassion for yourself in those moments where fear of any description is present. Hold the hand of your inner child, ACTION is the only thing that will shift any perception of fear, regardless the type of fear present.

10. Realize that you stand to be the creator of your own destiny, if you think you can you can

and if you think you can't you can't - transformation is very simplistic, don't complicate it.

It is time now to do yourself a favor and observe in future moments when you catch yourself stating you are fearful of failure or success. Get a sense of humor and take your power back, there is no reality to these statements unless you are choosing to feed them from your disconnected state! Nevertheless, do you understand the human nature?

Chapter 9: The Human Nature

The most powerful force in our world is undoubtedly our minds. It is the origin of all our thoughts, feelings, actions and behaviour. Simply put, whatever originates in it gets manifested on the conscious realm. Taking a daily activity such as TV watching, what actually happens when you want to change the channel? The thought comes to your mind first and then you pick up the remote and change it. Sometimes when you just do the action without thinking it essentially means that the thought originated subconsciously without you being aware of it.

You might have come across something that you don't particularly like. E.g. it could have been a commercial for a product of your dislike. This in turn involuntarily triggered the resultant reaction of changing the channel. From this, one can easily understand how impactful our subconscious is on our own actions. Accordingly, you solitarily understand why training the clout of the subliminal mind is so immensely important. Once this is done, there would be no stopping us in improving the quality of our lives beyond what we have ever thought possible.

If an individual can properly tap into and develop the powers of his subconscious mind, it can unearth all the potentials he has hidden. While many warn about the evils and dangers involved in this and it is good to know about the dark aspects of human psychology but focusing on such negativity only brings forth similar unfortunate consequences.

Hence, one should always look at the positive elements of the intuitive mind and go ahead to harness its abundant powers as a mode to self-improvement. If you are thinking this to be an extremely difficult and complicated process, you would be relieved to know that it is just the opposite. One knows how to exploit the command of his subconscious mind in drumming into and emerging wholly the concealed abilities that are laid inactive inside him. Likewise, undertaking this is not as grim as it is perceived to be. Over particular meek progressions specified beneath, you ought to be able to sort out this efficaciously.

One of the simplest ways in which you could guide your subconscious is with the technique of affirmation. By affirmation, we mean the ability to constantly remind your mind about a particular positive aspect of life for you to achieve the expected result. When an individual needs to finish a job that he finds no interest in, he usually senses a feeling of deep tiredness come over him and engulf him entirely.

How stress response and affirmation works best in such cases

One way this can be achieved is through constantly reminding oneself about how many benefits can be derived from performing the task. You could also look in the mirror and affirm clearly that you remain the absolute best person for the job. In fact, you are so good at the job the end result willpower be there as the ample knack exertion!

Avowals are ultimate in real establishment of developmental or accustomed vicissitudes on individuals. Presume, you are vexing to abandon smoldering, diminish imbibing or sojourn gorging too much, your unsurpassed method presumptuous would remain through the route of pronouncements. Scientific studies or whichever demonstration that are uninterruptedly recapping and prompting approximately to manually articulated or inscribed method, divert while hooked on the clout of your intuitive mind and in so doing create the prerequisite developmental transformation.

Post enthralling proposition is also additional mutual process for evolving the command of the subliminal observance. Customarily it is prompted beneath the administration of an eligible hypnotherapist nevertheless a distinct person is capable to prompt the analogous self-hypnosis using hypnosis audios. Brainwave synchronization through binaural rhythms is the 3rd procedure for subliminal mind command progress. In the discussed system, one is forced to receive dualistic different sound wave frequencies over both of his auricles therefore they can get into the mind and synchronize the two hemispheres. Thus, this marks in prompting a stupor comparable mental ailment, which is a prerequisite for effective communication between the conscious and subliminal fragment of one's brain.

Buddhist monks have mastered the art of levitation and invisibility showing to the world how the clout of the intuitive thoughts can be developed and taken to a different level altogether. Many would in fact call these feats as being supernatural. If an individual can control the power of his own subconscious, he will be able to control and manipulate matter in a subatomic level. Thus, you can even manipulate all events occurring around you and book and movies such as 'The Secret' only go on to corroborate the same through the Law of Attraction.

Thus, not only is it theoretically possible, but in essence it's a physical law that allows one to manifest in reality whatever it is that he wants in life just by communicating the same to his own subconscious. Amazing as it seems but the fact is that recent studies in the field of quantum psychics have come out with the very results that our age old religions of the world has been saying thousand years ago. Our lives or what we live in are nothing but the product of our own minds. Moreover, what ordinary people term as supernatural or psychic, all have been discussed by quantum physics.

Therefore, the influence of the intuitive mind can do wonders for you and your life. One should never underestimate it at all because apart from the usual required behavioral changes, it possesses the scope of transformation in your lifetime forever to something which you have only dreamt of in your most wonderful dreams.

The Subconscious or Intuitive Mind

Exploring how our subconscious works is the necessary first step behind realizing the various goals in our lives. Contrary to what most people believe, success in life does not so much depend on how smart we are or on whatever academic qualifications, which we may have achieved. Certainly, these are important contributing factors to success in our lives. However, the key here is developing a winning mentality, which would enable us to bring out the best of what we may have. Essentially, the human mind can be divided into two broad categories - the conscious mind and the subliminal mind. Essentially these two parts of the human mind co-exist with one another.

The conscious mind is the more familiar of the two, and we use it on a daily basis where we carry out cognitive functions such as making decisions or putting forward arguments. Thus, this part of the human mind constitutes to what most people would make use of to get about with life. To achieve success, it is necessary to move beyond this. On the other hand, the subconscious thoughts plays a key factor in our lives, in a comparatively unnoticeable fashion. This part of the human mind functions to regulate our bodily functions such as our heartbeat, our breathing, as well as the way in which we breathe. These are functions in life which we take for granted and barely notice.

How our subconscious works in our day-to-day lives is that it takes instructions from our conscious mind without questioning. Such instructions go through a process of repetition and affirmations. These are then realized as actions after such instructions are transmitted over to the conscious mind. Without such instructions brought forward over to the subconscious, no action would be taken and the subconscious would, as a result remain in a dormant state. Unlike the conscious mind, the subconscious has no ability to discern truth from falsity, as well as the reality from the imaginary.

Given such, it is important to surround our subconscious minds with positive affirmations. Negative affirmations would often be manifested as negative results as the intuitive mind transmits the undesired results over to the conscious mind, which then takes action, resulting in the undesirable effect being manifested in reality. Given then, we should take the effort each day to place positive affirmations in our lives. Start off by thinking positive thoughts each day while rooting out negative ones. After all, changes all start from somewhere. Instead of telling yourself that "It is my entire fault" when something fails, make the break by choosing positive statements such as "What can I learn from this experience". These may be trying at the very start. However, over time, you would be able to surround yourself with thoughts, words and actions that are positive in nature.

In a nutshell, our subconscious mind is a powerful tool that can affect us in many ways, be it the good or the bad. In any case, it is necessary for one to be able to master his or her subconscious through means of positive affirmations. Doing so will guarantee you happiness and allow you to achieve more out of your life.

Various Experiences

Individuals view environmental issues in various ways. Additionally, people contrarily determine the seriousness of environmental problems. Their worldviews, their opinions, are the basis of their understanding on how our planet operates and the proper ethical treatment of the environment and its life sources. Environmental issues pertaining to the "planetary management worldview" contend that humans are disconnected from nature. They propose there are no limitations pertaining to economic growth; that technical practical understanding and expertise will address any possible detriment to the environment. They also argue that nature produces human wants and needs; however, humans have managerial controls of earth's life support systems through our own ingenuity.

A second worldview considers that humans manage natural resources of our planet to our advantage and benefit. "Stewardship worldview" proponents suggest that we are ethically responsible in avoiding causing harm to the environment and life systems. However, concerning our economic growth and prosperity, according to the stewardship worldview and our desire to improve our living standards, humans should develop economically while practicing and maintaining environmental sustainability methods of economic growth.

Finally, those who practice the "environmental wisdom worldview," based primarily on the writings of Aldo Leopold, assert that nature exists for all living species. Humans rely on nature; they share the best and only way to exist on planet Earth. Humans must ethically practice the same time-proven, four scientific principles of sustainability that has been used on planet Earth for several billion years to avoid extinction. Personally, my environmental worldviews are bipolar and dichotic, that is, on one hand I ascribe to an environmental wisdom worldview-more succinctly, an earth-centered environmental worldview geared more towards deep ecology. However, on the other hand my faith is skewed, due in part from my perception of the lack of compassion, ethical behavior, intellect, and humility by many people.

Some of my studies of history have exposed me to how masses of cultures and population become prey and victims while at the mercy of human predators, environmental disasters, and impending death. The miniscule amount of insightful, enlightening, and innovative individuals throughout history are overshadowed by the myriad of self-centered, egotistic, power-driven characters who lead to devastating damage to the earth and its inhabitants, for example, Hitler, Mao Tse-tung, Stalin, Vlad the Impaler, Attila the Hun, Maximilien Robespierre, etc. It is my belief, multitudes of people follow the practices and latitudes of leaders with agendas that are contrary to environmental ethics; some are forced to obey and follow, whereas others shadow their leaders in the hope for survival or prosperity. I believe environmentalists are outnumbered.

Nonetheless, I am driven to "do what is right." Ironically, I sometimes consider the alternative viewpoint of leaving the environmental cleanup to future generations. It is easier to subscribe to this planetary management worldview. This is where ethics come into play. I recall as a child how wonderful trees were-how fascinating insects, dogs, and birds were-the glorious cloud formations, drifting and white snowfall, silver and blue rain, falling colorful leaves, meandering rivers flowing, and glistening lakes. No one had to teach me this fascination; it came naturally. I was a part of nature and nature was a part of me. Therefore, it is only morally true maintaining the viable acts projected by environmentalists and the unseen nature of life.

Chapter 10: Persistence and Originality

Persistence

As a professional network marketer, you are in a business that can be challenging at times. If you know the statistics, many would be network marketers quit after numerous failures. Only some are able to carry on despite all opposition and challenges until they obtain success.

If you are in a MIM company that has all the supports in place for you to be successful, but you have still been contemplating giving up, know that one of the major causes of failure is lack of persistence. If you want to achieve in your home business, you must arm yourself with a mindset of persistence no matter the obstacles you face.

Here are eight (8) tips regarding persistence, "Think and Grow Rich" that you can use to train yourself to be persistent.

1. **Have a definite purpose:** The first step and the most important is to know what you want. A powerful motive is the driving force in maintaining persistence to help you overcome difficulties.
2. **Maintain your desire**: Make sure you have a specific object or desire that will help you maintain your mindset of persistence.
3. Be self-reliant. Believe in your ability to carry out your plan. This will increase your persistence thermometer!
4. **Have definite plans**: You need to have organized plans to encourage persistence. It doesn't matter if they aren't that good to start with. Just make sure you have plans.
5. **Have an accurate knowledge base**: It helps if you know your goals and plans aren't based on guesswork, crazy theories, and the like. You must have knowledge based on experience and observation to encourage persistence.
6. **Cooperative:** A mindset of sympathy, understanding, and having a cooperative

attitude towards others helps you to develop persistence.

7. **Amp up that will power:** If you make the habit of concentrating your thoughts upon plan building so you can achieve your definite purpose, your persistence level will continue to increase.

8. **Be a creature of habit:** Persistence does not come automatically. It is the result of habit. Your mind absorbs your daily experiences. So, focus on never letting your persistent mindset go no matter the vicissitudes you go through in life as well as in your network marketing business.

Persistence is developed by doing the following the four steps below. Anyone can do these steps and it does not require any huge effort on your part.

1. Always have a definite purpose backed by a blazing desire to achieve your goals and dreams.

2. Always have a definite plan that you consistently act upon.
3. Have a mindset that stays closed to any type of negativity and discouraging influences. This can include negative statements and suggestion by your colleagues, friends, relatives, etc.
4. Make sure you have a friendly alliance with at least one person who consistently encourages you to act on your plan and purpose.

If you have been thinking of leaving your network marketing home business due to discouragement, take heart the above words. They do not require you to spend money, or a huge effort on your part. Develop a habit of persistence and you will never have to worry about falling into the ever-swelling ranks of the quitters.

The game of persistence: As writers we all think that our storyline, sentence structure and grammar is the best and it is only when we come up against an editor or critic that we are told that what we have written is either an illiterate mess, or amateurish and not to give up your day job. So if you are convinced that this is not so then who has the right to decide that which we have spent hours researching and correcting is unfit to be published?

If I told you that my latest novel is, "brilliant piece of fiction", and you have to buy it, will you? No, you would not because you do not know me and as far as you are concerned, I have no writing credibility. However, if a newspaper columnist or well-known book critic or even a famous presenter of a television program told you that a particular novel was a brilliant piece of fiction. Would you buy it? The probable outcome is that you would base on their recommendations, but what do they know about your taste in books? Very little and in fact it may have no impact. So what is the difference between the two?

How many of us have read books by a well-known author on the recommendation of a friend, book club, critic or press release only to find that the book we are supposed to be excited about is, as far as you are concerned, a boring excuse for a novel. Do well known writers survive because of their first success or because of publicity? You can compare it to the older entertainers who still keep appearing on our screens because of their past successes. If they had to start again, along with their aging skills, then many of them would be complete failures.

So what makes one book or story any better than the next? Is it the storyline, or prose or something else? Does a writer's first book lay a solid foundation on which to build upon for the next? How often have you read a story or novel and you enjoy the read only to learn later on that the book is viewed as a secondary work of art and will never be a best seller. Why does one person have the right to veto the work of another person when he is expressing only his own opinion? The clout of the written word has many users and non-more so than newspaper editors who can skillfully blend and bend a story to have a totally different meaning.

So are there many award winning novels dwelling in a forgotten folder, on some ones computer or a long forgotten manuscript stuffed carelessly in a drawer? The answer is yes there are, so how do you get them noticed and into print? Knowing the right people may help, submitting the manuscript to hundreds of publishers might help. If you are determined to be successful then you have to employ the good old standby called persistence. Use it to get your book out there and do not give up, without persistence you will not even have a chance of survival or success as a novelist.

To quote Mark Twain: The miracle, or the power, that elevates the few is to be found in their industry, application, and perseverance under the prompting of a brave, determined spirit.

Originality

Originality entails the art of being creative and innovative. On occasion it appears to me that all and sundry on the internet are busy copying each other. Consequently, this is not entirely a bad thing, but this perspective can also be limiting.

Creativity, fun, and originality can spice up your internet marketing. You certainly have to understand the concept of modeling, using the tried-and-true experience of someone else to cut corners, save time and money, and be on your way to depositing serious amounts of money into your bank account, you may wonder if this is entirely a significant and worthwhile maneuver. You see, there is no one quite like you.

You are unique

And while I'm not going so far as to recommend that you cleave entirely to fresh origination, I think that something worthwhile may come of letting your brain experiment with an original thesis. Economically, things could go either way.

Your original rendition of an old theme or your creation of something entirely new may or may not make an impact on your end-of-day receipts. However, from the perspective of personal satisfaction, there is a delight to creating a product that no-one else has made, proposing an idea that has never been pitched before, or stepping on a creative landmine in the middle of the night that keeps you on high alert for the rest of the nocturnal hours.

There is something unique about you, and when you roll it out, find it meets with an unexpected public frenzy because it offers unprecedented answer. You may feel more personally satisfied especially when achievements surpasses anything that you may earn. Of course, however, it's always wonderful to win a complete coup-and have your brilliance rewarded with numbers ending with numerous zeros-but that thrill is secondary to having the opportunity to be dazzling.

Perhaps a compromise is possible-between the bread-and-butter affiliate and resale right products and the methodology espoused by your adopted guru-and your own occasional creative flair. This way, you are assured of an income, and yet you have the freedom to play with an idea birthing in your brain alone, waiting to grow up enough to pull on its pants and go out there and do unbelievable electronic back flips to an amazed world.

Every unique idea in your brain needs to be treated with the respect due the dauphin of the kingdom. Treat the heir to the throne well, and he may very well surprise you with his empire-expanding vision. The internet can be more than a place where you make a great living; it can be a playground for a whirlwind of creativity, fun, and original contribution.

For example, an industrial design professional works on several aspects of an item, including the look and feel, materials used functionality etc. He makes the product useful and user friendly in its design and ensures that the user saves energy, time or labour by making use of the product.

An extremely creative line, this is a promising career option for creative individuals. A competent industrial designer can transform an inferior product into a multifunctional tool which can address numerous needs with great ease. To achieve any degree of success here, the designer should be very talented. The designer must be multi-talented to comprehend several aspects of the product and should be able to enhance it.

With technological advancements, sophisticated computer aided designing and simulations are possible now to provide the designer with an extra edge during the design of these products to meet the needs of the consumers. However, these technological tools will not substitute originality and innovative thinking that is needed in an industrial designer. Only for those with a knack for creativity and original thinking is this a good career opportunity.

Chapter 11: Getting Organized

Getting organized can help all people to lead a happier and more fulfilling life. This type of endeavor can lead to changes in many different areas of your life, as well as the relationships that you have. For you to be successful in bringing order to your life, one must give attention to both personal and professional interests. Time and finances are also important aspects of organization. Hopefully throughout this article we will examine the necessary things to be accomplished for effective organization.

Primarily, it is important to have a consistent work schedule. Thus, this must be organized with the help of a boss or supervisor. In addition, while at work, one should have a regimen that is easy to follow. An environment with these types of conditions will contribute to low stress levels.

Equally as important as work scheduling, is the time you spend with friends and family. Finding time in a busy week for those you care about is important in maintaining a balanced life. Moreover, time for loved ones will ensure that people know you care for them. In these busy times, people often overlook the necessity to make time for themselves. This alone time can assist individuals in personal reflections as well as recuperation. These are vital moments particularly for those who have many responsibilities.

Money does matter in our current society. Thus it is vital to have appropriate methods to organize your finances. This can help you learn to spend wisely, cut down on frivolous spending, and live within a budget that allows saving for the future. Living in an organized place can give an individual an increased sense of serenity. So as to achieve this, there are daily tasks and chores to be attended to. Additionally, for the sake of order, one must have a schedule of duties and proper storage at home. Vital papers and documents can be easily misplaced. Rental agreements, school transcripts, social security cards, passports, and birth certificates are just some of the items we need to keep in order. Careful organization with an at home filing system is highly recommended.

Planning for what is to come is also important for individuals hoping to feel more in control and organized. Making reachable goals and realistic plans about the future provides a sense of mental relief. Additionally, being organized about the future makes goals easier to reach. Organizing all of the aforementioned areas of your life can be a daunting task. However, there are many methods to achieving success. Making a list of things to do is a great approach. By organizing in this manner, and checking items off as you go, you will be on the path to order.

It should be clear to you now that the process of getting organized has a variety of moving parts. Putting work into one's personal and professional life is an essential part of the process. Personal time is an additional element to take note of. There are many other variables, but the key is to be organized in all aspects of your life if you want to maintain a peaceful mind. All that is left to do is to write a list and get started.

Chapter 12:
Indiscernible Laws and Their Tenacity

The human mind is made with a sense of understanding. This makes it possible to distinguish good from evil and normally without reading them from any school. These laws are invisible but are there and they have a great tenacity towards our life development.

What is the Law of Attraction?

For those not familiar with it, the Law of Attraction is a fundamental Law of the Universe. It is a law that applies particularly to conscious beings and it governs how events unfold in the lives of each and every one of us. No ordinary human being is immune from it.

The Law of Attraction states: "We attract whatever we choose to give our attention to whether wanted or unwanted". What this means is that most of the time we go through life focusing on problems that need to be solved and in so doing we actually create more problems. A good analogy is that of a magnet, which attracts other similar metal objects from a distance. The magnet does not have to try to attract: it just attracts.

In the same way we attract the likeness of what we are thinking about whether or not we try to. The exception is when we are asleep. If we are thinking about the lack of something, like money, then we attract more scarcity. If we think about something we love, then we attract whatever it is that we love.

The Sub Conscious Mind

The root of this invisible force of attraction is the sub conscious mind. The sub conscious mind is in a sense the magnet that does the attracting. The bit of our minds that gives us our daily awareness, the waking mind if you will, has limited capacity and is used only to sift through the millions of bits of data that, as conscious beings, we receive every second of the waking day. In doing so it uses the five senses to gather the most pertinent data around us and employs basic logic to enable us to negotiate the day safely.

The sub conscious mind on the other hand is by comparison almost infinite in capacity. If has been estimated that the sub conscious mind processes in excess of 40 million pieces of data per second compared with the waking consciousness which processes only around 40 thousand bits of data per second. So, although at any one moment in time we may appear to be fully aware of a particular scene, say a room full of clutter or the scene of a road accident, the sub conscious mind actually takes in a vast amount of additional information that we are not immediately aware of. This explains why people are able to remember minute detail under hypnosis compared to when they are in their normal waking state since hypnosis accesses the vast source of information in the sub-conscious mind.

Embed Your Dreams in the Sub Conscious Mind

Therefore, the key to achieving success and prosperity, if success and prosperity is what you desire, is to program your sub conscious mind to be in tune with your goals and aspirations. In other words we must influence the magnet that is the subliminal cognizance to attract the things we desire by making sure it prioritizes the information that relates to our desires when processing the vast amount of data it receives every second of the day. In practice this involves the use of the five key components of visualization to embed our goals in the sub conscious mind and in so doing the sub conscious mind will respond accordingly by attracting the objects of our desire to us in the manner described above. This process uses the techniques of visualization, reinforced by positive affirmations, to create a series of neurological networks in the brain that drive the goals into the sub conscious mind, which in turn responds by engendering the necessary thought patterns to direct us towards our goals.

Chapter 13: The Real Success

Are you looking for a real success? Are you sure you understand what you are looking for? Let briefly define a real success.

Real success

A real success can be shortly defined as a situation in life where a person can afford what he or she wants and possess the happiness that is upright without any influence but normal according to human life.

Some people have tried to gain wealth and joy from drugs. Therefore, this is practically unaccepted and can cause other types of diseases, physical or mental problems. As much as we need to be well-up or successful, we should not go for ways which leads us astray.

Most people think that is easy to fail than to succeed. Nothing is further from the truth. It is actually easier to succeed because the journey to success is one the most fantastic journey.

Here is a concrete example: they say that, for us to smile, we need to employ around 15 muscles in the face. To frown, we have to use more than 50. This shows that it takes more effort to smile than to frown. The same is true with success and failure. It would actually entail more effort on our part to fail than to succeed. This is because the ways of achieving success are actually beneficial to our physical, mental and spiritual wellbeing unlike ways to our failures.

The most important thing that successful people possess is faith. This includes faith in their abilities and faith that things will always turn out well. They say that if your mind can conceive your body can achieve. This is true. You will be surprised that by just believing in yourself, you will attract many opportunities that could ultimately lead you in reaching your goals. Faith will replace the fear that will attract negative things in your life.

Successful people always have a plan. And after you have made a plan you should stick to it as faithfully as possible. A plan is like a map that will lead you to the road of success. If your do not have a plan there is great possibility that you will get lost in the byways and highways of life. Making a clear plan will also help you increase you confidence which in turn will make you a stronger magnet for positive things. If you have a plan you will not also be easily swayed by wrong judgment and negative comments from other propel.

Discover your passion. Successful people are successful in what they do because they are genuinely passionate about it. These people do not merely work to have money or material success. They work because they love what they are doing and are passionate about it. Materials success is simply a byproduct of following their passion. How to discover your passion? Well it is very simple. Ask yourself this query, what are the things that truly excite you and what things do you really enjoy doing?

Learn from your mistakes and the mistakes of others. Successful people treat life as a learning experience. They are not ashamed of their mistakes. They also do not dwell in the unfortunate events that come their way. Instead, they draw valuable lessons from these experiences and use these lessons to propel them in achieving their goals. Successful people also take lessons from the mistakes of others. They are aware that they can avoid costly mistake by simply learning from the experiences of other people.

Be aware of your thoughts: Never ever think on a poverty level. Remember that nothing happens in your life unless your mind has pictured it first. Always try to think positive thoughts and say positive things. You will be amazed at the power that positive thoughts and words can bring to your life. Eliminate negative and limiting words from your vocabulary and replace them with positive and empowering ones.

Try to let go of the past: It is imperative to draw lessons from the past experiences. However, it wouldn't serve you well to dwell on them. Stand up where you have fallen and continue the journey. Letting go of the past will free yourself up from the burden that it brings and will free your life to the blessings that will come your way.

Keep on improving: Remember that life is an endless journey and that learning should never stop. Never even think that you have reached your potential. There is always room for change and each day is an opportunity to improve yourself in every aspect.

Always do your best: Remember that anything worth doing is worth doing well. Never ever turn out a mediocre work. Of course you can never be perfect but you can always strive to be excellent.

Enjoy life! Maintain a sense of humor: Do not take yourself too seriously. What seems like an insurmountable problem today would be a mere joke in the future. Take time to laugh. Enjoy and smell the flowers.

I want to be rich but how can I be wealthy and happy with small amount or no effort?

That is the wringer - "I want to be rich but how", is that which greatest number of people need answered, and they want it answered now! The thing is, initially you have to find out, what does it mean to "be rich and happy"? Some people possess all the funds in the world, nevertheless they're not satisfied. Still others need to dump the piggy bank each day, however they appear comparatively cheerful. Because to be rich and happy both requires all six basic individual needs to be met. And so you have to ask yourself, where are you on a ranking of 1-10, within each of the following basic individual needs:

1. **The need for certainty**.

We all have this need and we all find different ways to satisfy the requirement for positive assurance. Some of us fall into habitual schedules where we do the identical things each day, which meets this basic requirement. Others turn to their religion for something to depend on however we all have to feel like there's content in our life to keep us balanced, something we can count upon. When you look back in your life and understand that by some means you've always managed to pull yourself through the hurdles that life dished out, then you are more equipped later in life to feel certain relating to your own abilities. Of course, the greater life's difficulties that you have had to bear, the more assured you can feel about your own accomplishments.

2. **Just because God has a sense of humor, we also have a requirement for uncertainly.**

Many folks think that the secret to success is to make so much cash that you don't have to work anymore. But, if you check out people who have as a matter of fact done this, you'll see that honestly is NOT the secret to success. People that have all the money in the world without the need to go to work at all are especially depressed. Why? On account of they're bored.

That is how we find people habitually beginning a different career or opportunity after they gain their "rich goal" on account of they're bored out of their mind. All of us have a need for excitement and shake up, which is changeableness. That's how some large numbers of us can watch a movie that we have viewed aforetime, because we are sure that it's good, nevertheless we hope that we have forgotten only enough to make it changeable and surprising.

3. We have the need for importance.

Large numbers of us have a tendency to wander in this area and attempt to find importance by taking a "short cut", as with extreme force. A guy from the slums who was brought up with no feeling of importance about himself is apt to turn out this way, on account of, once he sticks a gun to your brain, suddenly he is important, and with a bunch less work than the guy who has chosen to acquire his Doctorate for significance. In some way, though, we all desire to "be noticed", if only just to seem to "be rich and happy". Nevertheless are we truly?

4. The 4th basic human requirement is the need for love.

All of us connect with something or somebody. It could be a life partner, kid, pet, or nature. However we really require to satisfy that fundamental requirement for interaction and love.

Be cautious here, because every now and then conflict between needs 3 & 4 can keep you from your ambition, "I want to be rich but how".

Just as needs 1 & 2 are in aversion of each other, so is the same complication between requirements 3 and 4. Some people who have acquired the life partner of their dreams frequently end up in divorce on account of one partner may grow to possess more importance over the other, and this depletes your own individual feelings of significance.

The above are the 4 basic needs, and we all manage to achieve them, whether abusive, or in a direction to help us grow and advance.

Naturally, when you can find a way to meet those needs to grow and evolve, then you are on your way to the true "success secrets of the rich and happy," because to be truly rich and happy depends on meeting requirements 5 & 6, which the greatest number of people rarely do.

Success Secrets of the Rich and Happy: "I want to be rich but how?" By fulfilling 5 & 6!

5. The need for development.

If you have chosen the precise way to meet your initial 4 basic human needs, then you're beginning to accomplish requirement number 5, the need for growth. Furthermore yes, this usually does take some time, but as they say, it's not the place one wants to go; it is the journey that is the real success to the secrets of the rich and happy.

6. Furthermore last, to really be rich and satisfied, you need to give back to the human race more than what you have received.

It is in giving that we receive. I am not simply speaking religious "gobbelty-gook" here. Note that, if you track the lifestyles of those who have really lived rewarding lives, you will notice that their business practice incorporated giving back to the human race more in worth than the dollar amount they accept. It's the rationalization why I am creating this post.

Since I believe that all of us are worthy of being wealthy and happy in our life, I'd like to show you the manner that I am doing it. Life is a journey, but it can be so rewarding once you begin training in what way or manner you can make money at the same time ~~while~~ you develop, evolve, and give back. All at the same time!

The 7 Secrets behind Success

A lot of people spend so much time developing skills that are not vital in ~~every person's~~ their lives. ~~Like,~~ Sure, it would be handy once in a while to know how to repair a broken lamp, ~~but~~ however it is not vital to one's existence. Some people master the art of repairing their car, but ~~we could~~ they also hire someone else to do ~~it for us~~ this job. We can learn how to sew an entire dress, ~~but~~ or we can buy ready to wear clothes from any clothing store. In short, there are some skills that are not essential if they are not applicable in your personal life.

But there are some people who cannot do without these skills because they are directly tied ~~up~~ to ~~them~~ their every day ~~of their~~ lives. Examples of these maybe knowing how to read and write or use a computer. These skills are vital when any person does another thing necessary - which is to earn a living. Of course, without a steady source of income, you will not have food to eat, a house to live in or clothes to wear.

For you to survive in any job, and to be successful in it, there are ~~simply~~ some simple skills that one cannot do without. You learn these skills over time, experience and constant practice. As you work on them more seriously, you increase your chances of being successful. *Here are 7 of the master skills any ambitious potentially-successful person must know.*

1. **How to prioritize and to manage time**: In any job, a schedule is essential. There must be a deadline or an allotted amount of time to accomplish tasks, otherwise, work will drag on forever without full completion. Success depends on effective action, and part and parcel of effectively is to be able to do task well within a schedule. A successful person

knows how to properly prioritize the more important things over the less vital. With the increasing amount of distractions surrounding us, time management is a much-needed skill - and definitely something any person must learn.

2. **Logical and informed decision making:** In life, you can never be successful without making decisions. It is a prerequisite to action - unless you plan on acting without thinking. Logical and sound decision making is knowing how to act based on the information and facts present. Remember - it is not about how quickly you can decide, but it is more on being able to make the best decisions based on the circumstances you are faced with.

3. **Basic accounting and money management:** Are you one of those who seem to constantly be in a quandary about where your money went? Do you leave the house with a pocketful of money, then be puzzled when you get home and discover how

much you have left? Well then, you can never be successful if you cannot even fully account for every dollar of your own personal money. Imagine being responsible for the funds of an entire company? Basic accounting, no matter how simple, is crucial to the individual success of a person. You must know how to spend money - wisely or on once in a while whims. Like they say, it does not matter how much you earn, but what matters is how much you save. Money, whether we admit it or not, keeps a roof over our heads, food in our bellies - which are some of man's most basic necessities. Knowing how to properly manage your money and income is a skill that not only helps one survive - it also is the key towards a sound and secure future.

4. **Effective communicating and negotiating:** To be successful, give people the information they need, rather than expect them to know what they should know. Don't rely on actions too much, because sometimes actions can be misinterpreted, and seen

within the context of the beholder. Instead of making people read your mind, master the art of proper and effective communication when miscommunication happens, be able to "negotiate" and defend your point within reason, without offending anyone. Always be honest and sincere when speaking - even when you must relay bad news. Remember the saying, it is better to be slapped with the truth than to be kissed with a lie.

5. **Relationship networking:** The key to survival nowadays in business is to be able to establish as many contacts and relationships as possible. They may be business relationships, friendships, or a client-supplier relationship. The ability to stay afloat relies on a business person's ability to earn the trust and confidence of as many people as possible.

6. **Positivity:** When people act according to how they feel, then their actions will be greatly influenced by their mindset. When you are optimistic and see the lesson behind

every failure, then you are always eager to get up and try again. When you are pessimistic and encounter failure, there's a big chance you will never get up after a fall. No matter how bad things may be, having positivity in your life will always make the world seem brighter and happier, and life is easier to live.

7. **Self-discipline:** Discipline is acting rightly when no one else is watching. Although it is a trait, it is also a skill which means, you can develop it over time with patient and sacrifice. It involves acting according to what is right, and giving up other more enjoyable things while being trusted to do a task. You have all the time in the world to do other things, but it takes self-discipline to give a task 100% of your attention when temptations abound. Self-discipline is ultimately that which will lead you towards success.

Conclusion

Self-confidence and self-esteem are the key things in every aspect to human life. Without either of them, your life is incomplete and unfocused or unproven. It's not very unusual to find people who have very little, even none, of this. If you're one of those people who want to improve on their self-confidence, you have to know that it always starts on the inside. Work out the issues that you have that cause you to have low confidence in the first place. Once you have worked these things out, then you can work on the outside appearances.

Nevertheless, when we understand our road blocks, emotional intelligence, persistence criterion, organizational criteria's and the secrets behind success, then we become able to achieve every objective because we will have built enough self-confidence and self-esteem.

Thank you for downloading this book!

CPSIA information can be obtained
at www.ICGtesting.com
Printed in the USA
LVOW13s2114290317
528981LV00010B/591/P